Pizza and Bread Cookbook

The Ultimate High-Tech Yet Simple Way to Enjoy Healthy Food Cooking Delicious Pizza and Bread's Craft Recipes For Your Grill and Oven

Chef Max Wilbur

The information herein is offered for informational purposes solely and is universal as so. The presentation of the information is without contract or any type of guarantee assurance.

The trademarks that are used are without any consent, and the publication of the trademark is without permission or backing by the trademark owner. All trademarks and brands within this book are for clarifying purposes only and are owned by the owners themselves, not affiliated with this document.

Table of Contents

INTRODUCTION

The Air Fryer Oven Grill is the perfect addition to any kitchen. It's a modern and stylish countertop cooking appliance that cooks faster and more efficiently than your standard electric or gas grill. It can be used on its own as a small griller or in conjunction with your larger countertop oven as an air fryer.

The Air Fryer has a unique design that allows you to cook a wide range of foods that your traditional stovetop or electric grills cannot handle. The large handle and spacious cooking area make it an attractive choice for anyone who wants to save time and space in your kitchen.

Step By Step Directions to Use the Air Fryer Grill

Step one:

Preheat the air fryer, add desired foods to the basket and close the lid. Turn the vent control knob to the "AIR DRY" position. Set the timer to cook for 20 minutes at 400°F (200°C). To use as a crockpot, set on low heat and cook for 8 hours or overnight.

Step two:

Remove food from the basket, drain excess oil, and serve. You may also season or marinate for further flavor enhancement before cooking (optional).

After cooking, keep calm in a covered container until ready to eat.

For best results, does not freeze or store in the refrigerator for longer than three days (if possible), as this will remove some of the oils from foods.

If you must store longer, at a low temperature (50 – 60 and use within 2-4 days. You may also season or marinate for further flavor enhancement before cooking (optional).

Tips and Tricks for Using the Air Fryer Grill

Use fresh ingredients that produce less moisture - consider no-oil salads or sautéed vegetables instead of fried.

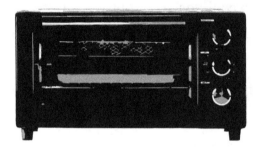

Care and maintenance

For best results, never immerse or submerge air fryer in water or any other liquid during use. Avoid letting water get on the heating element or fan, as this can cause damage to these parts and may affect their performance over time. There are no moving parts that will deteriorate over time; therefore, cleaning all removable parts will only require that they be wiped clean with a damp cloth. Use the only high-quality non-abrasive mild cleaner on non-removable components such as the door gasket or drip tray, as this can affect their performance. Use only silicone-based lubricants for cleaning your air fryer grill; do not use aerosol sprays in this area as these can damage delicate internal components. Avoid touching metal surfaces inside the appliance with your hands, as this can result in skin rashes or other issues

Use only mild dish detergent and hot water on a soft sponge to improve the longevity of the machine's finish.

It can cook up to 10 pounds of food in just 8 minutes!

The device cooks food by circulating air around the food. In just 30 minutes, you can have a delicious meal like never before. There are no dirty pans to clean and no wasted oil, making this device a win-win for both your health and your budget.

It is a tool that will revolutionize the way you cook. Unbox, prepare and start cooking.

The air fryer grill is easy to use, with the LCD panel on its side shows you the time and temperature settings. You can set up 8 different modes to cook your favorite foods. If you only want 2 minutes per side, use that mode; if you prefer 4 minutes per side, use that mode; if you wish to 6 minutes cooking time per side, then use the extended cooking mode.

Its 4 heat settings make sure your food doesn't burn before cooking is completed. It also has a power outlet to plug in your device and keep it safe from electricity spikes or power surges during those hot summer days. The food inside the air fryer cannot burn because of the non-stick pan plates used to make sure no oil gets on the food as you are cooking.

It also has a cool-touch exterior so that kids can use this without worry about burning their hands on the hot pan surface. The glass lid can be opened after it has been cooked so you can serve it in a bowl or plate without having to wait for the cool-down of the unit before serving.

This device is similar to other air fryers, except for how much air it can maintain at a time. This allows for more consistent cooking and better results every time.

With your Air Fryer Grill, you can prepare meals faster than ever before. You can use almost any cooking utensil to fry, bake, roast, broil, and much more. You can create gourmet meals in a fraction of the time it takes with traditional grill cookbooks or no cookers'

This product can be used for just about any type of food you can think of, so long as you are willing to try something new. It is easy to use and easy to clean, and uniquely can be used in the oven or on your grill or stovetop. The versatility will make you think about this tool more often than it took you to learn how great it is!!

Air Fryer Cooking Times

	Temp (°F)	Time (min)		Temp (°F)	Time (min)
Vegetables					
Asparagus (sliced 1-inch)	400°F	5	**Onions** (peart)	400°F	10
Beets (whole)	400°F	40	**Parsnips**	380°F	15
Broccoli (florets)	400°F	6	**Peppers** (1-inch chunks)	400°F	15
Brussels Sprouts (halved)	380°F	15	**Potatoes** (small baby, 1.5 lbs)	400°F	15
Carrots (sliced 1/2-inch)	380°F	15	**Potatoes** (1-inch chunks)	400°F	12
Cauliflower (florets)	400°F	12	**Potatoes** (baked whole)	400°F	40
Com on the cob	390°F	6	**Squash** (1/2-inch chunks)	400°F	12
Eggplant (11/2-inch cubes)	400°F	15	**Sweet Potato**	380°F	30 to 35
Fennel (quartered)	370°F	15	**Tomatoes** (cherry)	400°F	4
Green Beans	400°F	5	**Tomatoes** (halves)	350°F	10
Kale leaves	250°F	12	**Zucchini** (1/2-inch sticks)	400°F	12
Mushrooms (sliced 1/4-inch)	400°F	5			

Chicken

Breasts, bone in (1.25 lbs.)	370°F	25	**Legs, bone in** (1.75 lbs.)	380°F	30
Breasts, boneless (4 oz.)	380°F	12	**Wings** (2 lbs.)	400°F	12
Drumsticks (2.5 lbs.)	370°F	20	**Game Hen** (halved - 2 lbs.)	390°F	20
Thighs, bone In (2 lbs.)	380°F	22	**Whole Chicken** (6.5 lbs.)	360°F	75
Thighs, boneless (1.5 lbs.)	380°F	18 to 20	**Tenders**	360°F	8 to 10

Beef

Burger (4 oz.)	370°F	16 to 20	**Meatballs** (3-inch)	380°F	10
Filet Mignon (8 oz.)	400°F	18	**Ribeye, bone In** (1-inch, 8 oz.)	400°F	10 to 15
Flank Steak (1.5 lbs.)	400°F	12	**Sirloin steaks** (1-inch, 12 oz.)	400°F	9 to 14
London Broil (2 lbs.)	400°F	20 to 28	**Beef Eye Round Roast** (4 lbs.)	390°F	45 to 55
Meatballs (1-inch)	380°F	7			

Pork and Lamb

Loin (2 lbs.)	360°F	55	**Bacon** (thick cut)	400°F	6 to 10

Pork Chops, bone in (1-inch, 6.5 oz.)	400°F	12	**Sausages**	380°F	15
Tenderloin (1 lb.)	370°F	15	**Lamb Loin Chops** (1-	400°F	8 to 12
Bacon (regular)	400°F	5 to 7	**Rack of lamb** (1.5 - 2 lbs.)	380°F	22
Fish and Seafood					
Calamari (8 oz.)	400°F	4	**Tuna steak**	400°F	7 to 10
Fish Fillet (1-inch, 8oz.)	400°F	10	**Scallops**	400°F	5 to 7
Salmon, fillet (6oz.)	380°F	12	**Shrimp**	400°F	5
Swordfish steak	400°F	10			
Frozen Foods					
Onion Rings (12 oz.)	400°F	8	**Fish Sticks** (10 oz.)	400°F	10
Thin French Fries (20 oz.)	400°F	14	**Fish Fillets** (1/2-inch, 10	400°F	14
Thick French Fries (17 oz.)	400°F	18	**Chicken Nuggets** (12	400°F	10
Mozzarella Sticks (11 oz.)	400°F	8	**Breaded Shrimp**	400°F	9
Pot Stickers (10 oz.)	400°F	8			

Pizza and Bread Recipes

Crisp Avocado and Slaw Tacos

Preparation time: 15 minutes

Cooking time: 6 minutes

Servings 4

Ingredients:

- 1/4 cup all-purpose flour
- 1/4 teaspoon salt,
- 1/4 teaspoon ground black pepper
- 2 large egg whites
- 11/4 cups panko bread crumbs
- 2 tablespoons olive oil
- 2 avocados, peeled and halved, cut into 1/2-inch-thick slices
- 1/2 small red cabbage, thinly sliced
- 1 deseeded jalapeño, thinly sliced

- 2 green onions, thinly sliced
- 1/2 cup cilantro leaves
- 1/4 cup mayonnaise
- Juice and zest of 1 lime
- 4 corn tortillas, warmed
- 1/2 cup sour cream
- Cooking spray

Directions:

1. Set the air fryer basket with cooking spray.
2. Pour the flour in a large bowl and sprinkle with salt and black pepper, and then stir to mix well.
3. Whisk the egg whites in a separate bowl. Combine the panko with olive oil on a shallow dish.
4. Dredge the avocado slices in the bowl of flour, then into the egg to coat. Shake the excess off, and then roll the slices over the panko.
5. Set the avocado slices in a single layer in the basket and spritz the cooking spray.
6. Slide the basket into the air fryer. Cook at the corresponding preset mode or Air Fry at 400F (205C) for 6 minutes.
7. Flip the slices halfway through with tongs.
8. When cooking is complete, the avocado slices should be tender and lightly browned.

9. Combine the cabbage, jalapeño, onions, cilantro leaves, mayo, lime juice and zest, and a touch of salt in a separate large bowl. Toss to mix well.

10. Unfold the tortillas on a clean work surface, then spread with cabbage slaw and air fried avocados. Top with sour cream and serve.

Nutrition: Calories 350 Fat 15 g Carbohydrates 3 g Sugar 1 g Protein 44 g Cholesterol 0 mg

Eggplant Subs

Preparation time: 15 minutes

Cooking time: 12 minutes

Servings: 3 subs

Ingredients:

- 6 peeled eggplant slices (about 1/2 inch thick and 3 inches in diameter)
- 1/4 cup jarred pizza sauce
- 6 tablespoons grated Parmesan cheese
- 3 Italian sub rolls, split open lengthwise, warmed
- Cooking spray

Directions:

1. Set the air fryer basket with cooking spray.
2. Arrange the eggplant slices in the basket and spritz with cooking spray.
3. Slide the basket into the air fryer. Cook at the corresponding preset mode or Air Fry at 350F (180C) for 10 minutes.

4. Flip the slices halfway through the cooking time.

5. When cooked, the eggplant slices should be lightly wilted and tender.

6. Divide and spread the pizza sauce and cheese on top of the eggplant slice

7. Slide the basket into the air fryer. Cook at the corresponding preset mode or Air Fry at 375F (190C) for 2 minutes. When cooked, the cheese will be melted.

8. Assemble each sub roll with two slices of eggplant and serve immediately.

Nutrition: Calories 256 Fat 13.3 g Carbohydrates 0 g Sugar 0 g Protein 34.5 g Cholesterol 78 mg

Green Bean, Mushroom, and Chickpea Wraps

Preparation time: 15 minutes

Cooking time: 9 minutes

Servings 4

Ingredients

- 8 ounces (227 g) green beans
- 2 portobello mushroom caps, sliced
- 1 large red pepper, sliced
- 2 tablespoons olive oil, divided
- 1/4 teaspoon salt
- 1 (15-ounce / 425-g) can chickpeas, drained
- 3 tablespoons lemon juice
- 1/4 teaspoon ground black pepper
- 4 (6-inch) whole-grain wraps
- 4 ounces (113 g) fresh herb or garlic goat cheese, crumbled
- 1 lemon, cut into wedges

Directions:s

1. Add the green beans, mushrooms, red pepper to a large bowl. Set with 1 tablespoon olive oil and season with salt. Toss until well coated.
2. Transfer the vegetable mixture to a baking pan.
3. Slide the pan into the air fryer. Cook at the corresponding preset mode or Air Fry at 400F (205C) for 9 minutes.
4. Stir the vegetable mixture three times during cooking.
5. When cooked, the vegetables should be tender.
6. Meanwhile, mash the chickpeas with lemon juice, pepper and the remaining 1 tablespoon oil until well blended
7. Unfold the wraps on a clean work surface. Spoon the chickpea mash on the wraps and spread all over.
8. Divide the cooked veggies among wraps. Sprinkle 1 ounce crumbled goat cheese on top of each wrap. Fold to wrap. Squeeze the lemon wedges on top and serve.

Nutrition: Calories 136 Fat 12.6 g Carbohydrates 4.1 g Sugar 0.5 g Protein 10.3 g Cholesterol 88 mg

Korean Beef Tacos

Preparation time: 1 hour 15 minutes

Cooking time: 12 minutes

Servings 6

Ingredients:

- 2 tablespoons gochujang
- 1 tablespoon soy sauce
- 2 tablespoons sesame seeds
- 2 teaspoons minced fresh ginger
- 2 cloves garlic, minced
- 2 tablespoons toasted sesame oil
- 2 teaspoons sugar
- 1/2 teaspoon kosher salt
- 11/2 pounds (680 g) thinly sliced beef chuck

- 1 medium red onion, sliced
- 6 corn tortillas, warmed
- 1/4 cup chopped fresh cilantro
- 1/2 cup kimchi
- 1/2 cup chopped green onions

Directions:

1. Combine the gochujang, soy sauce, sesame seeds, ginger, garlic, sesame oil, sugar, and salt in a large bowl. Stir to mix well.
2. Dunk the beef chunk in the large bowl. Press to submerge, then wrap the bowl in plastic and refrigerate to marinate for at least 1 hour.
3. Remove the beef chunk from the marinade and transfer to the air fryer basket. Add the onion to the basket.
4. Slide the basket into the air fryer. Cook at the corresponding preset mode or Air Fry at 400F (205C) for 12 minutes.
5. Set the mixture halfway through the cooking time.
6. When cooked, the beef will be well browned.
7. Unfold the tortillas on a clean work surface, and then divide the fried beef and onion on the tortillas. Spread the cilantro, kimchi, and green onions on top.
8. Serve immediately.

Nutrition: Calories: 373 Total Fat: 21g Saturated Fat: 3g Cholesterol: 75mg Sodium: 218mg Carbohydrates: 13g Fiber: 1g Protein: 34g

Lamb Hamburgers

Preparation time: 15 minutes

Cooking time: 16 minutes

Servings 4 burgers

Ingredients:

- 11/2 pounds (680 g) ground lamb
- 1/4 cup crumbled feta
- 11/2 teaspoons tomato paste
- 11/2 teaspoons minced garlic
- 1 teaspoon ground dried ginger
- 1 teaspoon ground coriander
- 1/4 teaspoon salt
- 1/4 teaspoon cayenne pepper
- 4 kaiser rolls or hamburger buns, split open lengthwise, warmed
- Cooking spray

Directions:

1. Set the air fryer basket with cooking spray.
2. Combine all the ingredients, except for the buns, in a large bowl. Coarsely stir to mix well.
3. Shape the mixture into four balls, and then pound the balls into four 5-inch diameter patties.
4. Arrange the patties in the basket and spritz with cooking spray.
5. Slide the basket into the air fryer. Cook at the corresponding preset mode or Air Fry at 375F (190C) for 16 minutes.
6. Set the patties halfway through the cooking time.
7. When cooking is processed, the patties should be well browned.
8. Assemble the buns with patties to make the burgers and serve immediately.

Nutrition: Calories 260 Fat 13 g Carbohydrates 1 g Sugar 0 g Protein 35 g Cholesterol 142 mg

Mexican Chicken Burgers

Preparation time: 15 minutes

Cooking time: 20 minutes

Servings 6 to 8

Ingredients:

- 4 skinless and boneless chicken breasts
- 1 small head of cauliflower, sliced into florets
- 1 jalapeño pepper
- 3 tablespoons smoked paprika
- 1 tablespoon thyme
- 1 tablespoon oregano
- 1 tablespoon mustard powder
- 1 teaspoon cayenne pepper
- 1 egg
- Salt and ground black pepper, to taste
- 2 tomatoes, sliced
- 2 lettuce leaves, chopped

- 6 to 8 brioche buns, sliced lengthwise
- 1/3 cup taco sauce
- Cooking spray

Directions:

1. Set the air fryer basket with cooking spray. Set aside.
2. In a blender, add the cauliflower florets, jalapeño pepper, paprika, thyme, oregano, mustard powder and cayenne pepper and blend until the mixture has a texture similar to bread crumbs.
3. Transfer 1/3 of the cauliflower mixture to a medium bowl and set aside. Set the egg in a different bowl and set aside.
4. Add the chicken breasts to the blender with remaining cauliflower mixture. Sprinkle with salt and pepper. Blend until finely chopped and well mixed.
5. Remove the mixture from the blender and form into 6 to 8 patties. One by one, dredge each patty in the reserved cauliflower mixture, then into the egg. Dip them in the cauliflower mixture again for additional coating.
6. Put the coated patties into the basket and spritz with cooking spray.
7. Slide the basket into the air fryer. Cook at the corresponding preset mode or Air Fry at 350F (180C) for 20 minutes.
8. Set the patties halfway through the cooking time.

9. When cooking is processed, the patties should be golden and crispy.

10. Transfer the patties to a clean work surface and assemble with the buns, tomato slices, chopped lettuce leaves and taco sauce to make burgers. Serve and enjoy.

Nutrition: Calories: 147 Total Fat: 5g Saturated Fat: 1g Cholesterol: 71mg Sodium: 244mg Carbohydrates: 10g Fiber: 4g Protein: 16g

Montreal Beef Burgers

Preparation time: 15 minutes

Cooking time: 10 minutes

Servings 4

Ingredients:

- 1 teaspoon cumin seeds
- 1 teaspoon mustard seeds
- 1 teaspoon coriander seeds
- 1 teaspoon dried minced garlic
- 1 teaspoon dried red pepper flakes
- 1 teaspoon kosher salt
- 2 teaspoons ground black pepper
- 1 pound (454 g) 85% lean ground beef
- 2 tablespoons Worcestershire sauce
- 4 hamburger buns
- Mayonnaise, for serving
- Cooking spray

Directions:

1. Set the air fryer basket with cooking spray.
2. Put the seeds, garlic, red pepper flakes, salt, and ground black pepper in a food processor. Pulse to coarsely ground the mixture.
3. Put the ground beef in a large bowl. Pour in the seed mixture and drizzle with Worcestershire sauce. Stir to mix well.
4. Set the mixture into four parts and shape each part into a ball, then bash each ball into a patty. Arrange the patties in the basket.
5. Slide the basket into the air fryer. Cook at the corresponding preset mode or Air Fry at 350F (180C) for 10 minutes.
6. Flip the patties with tongs halfway through the cooking time.
7. When cooked, the patties will be well browned.
8. Assemble the buns with the patties, and then drizzle the mayo over the patties to make the burgers. Serve immediately.

Nutrition: Calories 184 Fat 11 g Carbohydrates 5 g Sugar 1 g Protein 12 g Cholesterol 0 mg

Mushroom and Cabbage Spring Rolls

Preparation time: 20 minutes

Cooking time: 14 minutes

Servings 14

Ingredients:

- 2 tablespoons vegetable oil
- 4 cups sliced Napa cabbage
- 5 ounces (142 g) shiitake mushrooms, diced
- 3 carrots, cut into thin matchsticks
- 1 tablespoon minced fresh ginger
- 1 tablespoon minced garlic
- 1 bunch scallions
- 2 tablespoons soy sauce
- 1 (4-ounce / 113-g) package cellophane noodles

- 1/4 teaspoon cornstarch
- 1 (12-ounce / 340-g) package frozen spring roll wrappers, thawed
- Cooking spray

Directions:s

1. Warmth the olive oil in a nonstick skillet until shimmering.
2. Add the cabbage, mushrooms, and carrots and sauté for 3 minutes or until tender.
3. Add the ginger, garlic, and scallions and sauté for 1 minutes or until fragrant.
4. Mix in the soy sauce and turn off the heat. Discard any liquid remains in the skillet and allow to cool.
5. Bring a pot of water to a boil, then turn off the heat and pour in the noodles. Let sit until the noodles are al dente. Transfer 1 cup of the noodles in the skillet and toss with the cooked vegetables. Reserve the remaining noodles for other use.
6. Set the cornstarch in a small dish of water, and then place the wrappers on a clean work surface. Dab the edges of the wrappers with cornstarch.
7. Scoop up 3 tablespoons of filling in the center of each wrapper, and then fold the corner in front of you over the filling. Tuck the wrapper under the filling, and then fold the corners on both sides into the center. Keep rolling to seal the wrapper. Repeat with remaining wrappers.

8. Set the air fryer basket with cooking spray. Arrange the wrappers in the basket and spritz with cooking spray.

9. Slide the basket into the air fryer. Cook at the corresponding preset mode or Air Fry at 400F (205C) for 10 minutes.

10. Flip the wrappers halfway through the cooking time.

11. When cooking is complete, the wrappers will be golden brown.

12. Serve immediately.

Nutrition: Calories 325 Fat 16.5 g Carbohydrates 0.4 g Sugar 0.2 g Protein 41.4 g Cholesterol 131 mg

Philly Cheesesteaks

Preparation time: 20 minutes

Cooking time: 20 minutes

Servings 2

Ingredients:

- 12 ounces (340 g) boneless rib-eye steak, sliced thinly
- 1/2 teaspoon Worcestershire sauce
- 1/2 teaspoon soy sauce
- Kosher salt and black pepper, to taste
- 1/2 green bell pepper, stemmed, deseeded, and thinly sliced
- 1/2 small onion, halved and thinly sliced
- 1 tablespoon vegetable oil
- 2 soft hoagie rolls, split three-fourths of the way through
- 1 tablespoon butter, softened
- 2 slices provolone cheese, halved

Directions:

1. Combine the steak, Worcestershire sauce, soy sauce, salt, and ground black pepper in a large bowl. Toss to coat well. Set aside.

2. Combine the bell pepper, onion, salt, ground black pepper, and vegetable oil in a separate bowl. Toss to coat the vegetables well.

3. Pour the steak and vegetables in the air fryer basket.

4. Slide the basket into the air fryer. Cook at the corresponding preset mode or Air Fry at 400F (205C) for 15 minutes.

5. When cooked, the steak will be browned and vegetables will be tender. Transfer them on a plate. Set aside.

6. Brush the hoagie rolls with butter and place in the basket.

7. Slide the basket in the air fryer and toast for 3 minutes. When done, the rolls should be lightly browned.

8. Transfer the rolls to a clean work surface and divide the steak and vegetable mix in between the rolls. Spread with cheese. Put the stuffed rolls back in the basket.

9. Cook for 2 minutes. Bring the basket back to the air fryer. When done, the cheese should be melted.

10. Serve immediately.

Nutrition: Calories 122 Total Fat 7.8 g Saturated Fat 1.2 g Cholesterol 0 mg Sodium 81 mg Total Carbs 12.7 g Fiber 3.5 g Sugar 6.8g Protein 4.3 g

Pork and Cabbage Gyoza

Preparation time: 10 minutes

Cooking time: 10 minutes

Servings 48

Ingredients:

- 1 pound (454 g) ground pork
- 1 head Napa cabbage (about 1 pound / 454 g), sliced thinly and minced
- 1/2 cup minced scallions
- 1 teaspoon minced fresh chives
- 1 teaspoon soy sauce
- 1 teaspoon minced fresh ginger
- 1 tablespoon minced garlic
- 1 teaspoon granulated sugar
- 2 teaspoons kosher salt
- 48 to 50 wonton or dumpling wrappers
- Cooking spray

Directions:

1. Set the air fryer basket with cooking spray. Set aside.
2. Make the filling: Combine all the ingredients, except for the wrappers in a large bowl. Stir to mix well.
3. Unfold a wrapper on a clean work surface, and then dab the edges with a little water. Scoop up 2 teaspoons of the filling mixture in the center.
4. Make the gyoza: Fold the wrapper over to filling and press the edges to seal. Pleat the edges if desired. Repeat with remaining wrappers and fillings.
5. Arrange the gyozas in the basket and spritz with cooking spray.
6. Slide the basket into the air fryer. Cook at the corresponding preset mode or Air Fry at 360F (182C) for 10 minutes.
7. Flip the gyozas halfway through the cooking time.
8. When cooked, the gyozas will be golden brown.
9. Serve immediately.

Nutrition: Calories 230 Fat 11 g Carbohydrates 2 g Sugar 0.2 g Protein 27 g Cholesterol 79 mg

Pork and Carrot Momos

Preparation time: 20 minutes

Cooking time: 20 minutes

Servings 4

Ingredients:

- 2 tablespoons olive oil
- 1 pound (454 g) ground pork
- 1 shredded carrot
- 1 onion, chopped
- 1 teaspoon soy sauce
- 16 wonton wrappers
- Salt and ground black pepper, to taste
- Cooking spray

Directions:

1. Warmth the olive oil in a nonstick skillet until shimmering.

2. Add the ground pork, carrot, onion, soy sauce, salt, and ground black pepper and sauté for 10 minutes or until the pork is well browned and carrots are tender.

3. Unfold the wrappers on a clean work surface, and then divide the cooked pork and vegetables on the wrappers. Set the edges around the filling to form momos. Nip the top to seal the momos.

4. Arrange the momos in the air fryer basket and spritz with cooking spray.

5. Slide the basket into the air fryer. Cook at the corresponding preset mode or Air Fry at 320F (160C) for 10 minutes.

6. When cooking is complete, the wrappers will be lightly browned.

7. Serve immediately.

Nutrition: Calories 290 Fat 10 g Carbohydrates 3 g Sugar 0.3 g Protein 40 g Cholesterol 0 mg

Pork Sliders

Preparation time: 10 minutes

Cooking time: 14 minutes

Servings 6

Ingredients:

- 1 pound (454 g) ground pork
- 1 tablespoon Thai curry paste
- 11/2 tablespoons fish sauce
- 1/4 cup thinly sliced scallions,
- 2 tablespoons minced peeled fresh ginger
- 1 tablespoon light brown sugar
- 1 teaspoon ground black pepper
- 6 slider buns, split open lengthwise, warmed
- Cooking spray

Directions:

1. Set the air fryer basket with cooking spray.

2. Combine all the ingredients, except for the buns in a large bowl. Stir to mix well.

3. Divide and shape the mixture into six balls, then bash the balls into six 3-inch-diameter patties.

4. Arrange the patties in the basket and spritz with cooking spray.

5. Slide the basket into the air fryer. Cook at the corresponding preset mode or Air Fry at 375F (190C) for 14 minutes.

6. Set the patties halfway through the cooking time.

7. When cooked, the patties should be well browned.

8. Assemble the buns with patties to make the sliders and serve immediately.

Nutrition: Calories 122 Total Fat 7.8 g Saturated Fat 1.2 g Cholesterol 0 mg Sodium 81 mg Total Carbs 12.7 g Fiber 3.5 g Sugar 6.8g Protein 4.3 g

Potato and Pea Samosas with Chutney

Preparation time: 30 minutes

Cooking time: 22 minutes

Servings: 16 samosas

Ingredients:

Dough:

- 4 cups all-purpose flour,
- 1/4 cup plain yogurt
- 1/2 cup cold unsalted butter
- 2 teaspoons kosher salt
- 1 cup ice water

Filling:

- 2 tablespoons vegetable oil
- 1 onion, diced
- 11/2 teaspoons coriander
- 11/2 teaspoons cumin

- 1 clove garlic, minced
- 1 teaspoon turmeric
- 1 teaspoon kosher salt
- 1/2 cup peas, thawed if frozen
- 2 cups mashed potatoes
- 2 tablespoons yogurt
- Cooking spray

Chutney:

- 1 cup mint leaves, lightly packed
- 2 cups cilantro leaves, lightly packed
- 1 green Chili pepper, deseeded and minced
- 1/2 cup minced onion
- Juice of 1 lime
- 1 teaspoon granulated sugar
- 1 teaspoon kosher salt
- 2 tablespoons vegetable oil

Directions:

1. Put the flour, yogurt, butter, and salt in a food processor. Pulse to combine until grainy. Pour in the water and pulse until a smooth and firm dough forms.

2. Transfer the dough on a clean and lightly floured working surface. Knead the dough and shape it into a ball. Cut in half and flatten the halves into 2 discs. Wrap them in plastic and let sit in refrigerator until ready to use.

3. Meanwhile, make the filling: Warmth the vegetable oil in a saucepan over medium heat.

4. Attach the onion and sauté for 5 minutes or until lightly browned.

5. Add the coriander, cumin, garlic, turmeric, and salt and sauté for 2 minutes or until fragrant.

6. Add the peas, potatoes, and yogurt and stir to combine well. Turn off the heat and allow cooling.

7. Meanwhile, combine the ingredients for the chutney in a food processor. Pulse to mix well until glossy. Set the chutney in a bowl and refrigerate until ready to use.

8. Make the samosas: Remove the dough discs from the refrigerator and cut each disc into 8 parts. Shape each part into a ball, and then roll the ball into a 6-inch circle. Divide the circle in half and roll each half into a cone.

9. Scoop up 2 tablespoons of the filling into the cone; press the edges of the cone to seal and form into a triangle. Repeat with remaining dough and filling.

10. Set the air fryer basket with cooking spray. Arrange the samosas in the basket and spritz with cooking spray.

11. Slide the basket into the air fryer. Cook at the corresponding preset mode or Air Fry at 360F (182C) for 15 minutes.

12. Flip the samosas halfway through the cooking time.

13. When cooked, the samosas will be golden brown and crispy.

14. Serve the samosas with the chutney.

Nutrition: Calories: 626kcal Carbs: 10g Protein: 72g Fat: 31g.

Friendly Bagels

Preparation time: 20 minutes

Cooking time: 18 minutes

Servings 4

Ingredients

- 1 cup self-rising flour
- 1 cup low Greek yogurt
- 1 egg

Directions:

1. Mix together yogurt and flour until becomes a ball of dough.
2. Place ball of dough on a flat surface and cover with flour.
3. Separate into 4 balls.
4. Roll each ball into a long rope
5. Shape into a bagel form.
6. Whisk egg.
7. Coat each bagel with an egg wash and any toppings.

8. Place in air fryer or ninja basket

9. Place on 350 for 10 minutes.

Nutrition: Calories: 548 Fat: 20.7g Protein: 46g Carbs: 1.2 g

Crab Toasts

Preparation time: 10 minutes

Cooking time: 5 minutes

Servings 15 to 18 toasts

Ingredients:

- 1 (6-ounce / 170-g) can flaked crabmeat, well drained
- 3 tablespoons light mayonnaise
- 1/4 cup shredded Parmesan cheese
- 1/4 cup shredded Cheddar cheese
- 1 teaspoon Worcestershire sauce
- 1/2 teaspoon lemon juice
- 1 loaf artisan bread, French bread, or baguette, cut into 3/8inch-thick slices

Directions:s

1. In a large bowl, merge together all the ingredients except the bread slices.
2. On a clean work surface, lay the bread slices. Spread 1/2 tablespoon of crab mixture onto each slice of bread.
3. Arrange the bread slices in the air fryer basket.
4. Slide the basket into the air fryer. Cook at the corresponding preset mode or Air Fry at 360F (182C) for 5 minutes.
5. When cooking is complete, the tops should be lightly browned. Remove from the air fryer. Serve warm.

Nutrition: Calories 515 Fat 33 g Carbohydrates 2 g Sugar 0 g Protein 45 g Cholesterol 0 mg

Shrimp and Sesame Seed Toasts

Preparation time: 15 minutes

Cooking time: 8 minutes

Servings 4 to 6

Ingredients:

- 1/2 pound (227 g) raw shrimp, peeled and deveined
- 1 egg, beaten
- 2 scallions, chopped, plus more for garnish
- 2 tablespoons chopped fresh cilantro
- 2 teaspoons grated fresh ginger
- 1 to 2 teaspoons sriracha sauce
- 1 teaspoon soy sauce
- 1/2 teaspoon toasted sesame oil
- 6 slices thinly sliced white sandwich bread
- 1/2 cup sesame seeds
- Cooking spray
- Thai chili sauce, for serving

Directions:

1. In a food processor, attach the shrimp, egg, scallions, cilantro, ginger, sriracha sauce, soy sauce and sesame oil, and pulse until chopped finely. Transfer the shrimp mixture to a bowl.
2. On a clean work surface, cut the crusts off the sandwich bread. Using a brush, generously brush one side of each slice of bread with shrimp mixture.
3. Put the sesame seeds on a plate. Press bread slices, shrimp-side down, into sesame seeds to coat evenly. Cut each slice diagonally into quarters.
4. Set the air fryer basket with cooking spray. Spread the coated slices in a single layer in the air fryer basket.
5. Slide the basket into the air fryer. Cook at the corresponding preset mode or Air Fry at 400F (205C) for 8 minutes.
6. Flip the bread slices halfway through.
7. When cooking is processed, they should be golden and crispy. Detach from the air fryer to a plate and let cool for 5 minutes. Top with the chopped scallions and serve warm with Thai chili sauce.

Nutrition: Calories 525 Fat 25g Carbs 34g Protein 41g

Bourbon French toast

Preparation time: 15 minutes

Cooking time: 6 minutes

Servings 4

Ingredients:

- 2 large eggs
- 2 tablespoons water
- 2/3 cup whole or 2% milk
- 1 tablespoon butter, melted
- 2 tablespoons bourbon
- 1 teaspoon vanilla extract
- 8 (1-inch-thick) French bread slices
- Cooking spray

Directions:

1. Set the air fryer basket with parchment paper and spray it with cooking spray.

2. Beat the eggs with the water in a shallow bowl until combined. Add the milk, melted butter, bourbon, and vanilla and stir to mix well.

3. Dredge 4 slices of bread in the batter, turning to coat both sides evenly. Transfer the bread slices onto the parchment paper.

4. Slide the basket into the air fryer. Cook at the corresponding preset mode or Air Fry at 320F (160C) for 6 minutes.

5. Flip the slices halfway through the cooking time.

6. When cooking is complete, the bread slices should be nicely browned.

7. Detach from the air fryer to a plate and serve warm.

Nutrition: Calories: 67 Fat: 8gProtein: 3g Carbs: 1 g

Cheesy Ham Toast

Preparation time: 5 minutes

Cooking time: 6 minutes

Serves: 1

Ingredients:

- 1 slice bread
- 1 teaspoon butter
- 1 egg
- Salt and ground black pepper, to taste

- 2 teaspoons diced ham
- 1 tablespoon Cheddar cheese

Directions:

1. Set a clean work surface; use a 21/2-inch biscuit cutter to make a hole in the center of the bread slice with about 1/2-inch of bread remaining.

2. Scatter the butter on both sides of the bread slice. Set the egg into the hole and season with salt and pepper to taste. Transfer the bread to the air fryer basket.

3. Slide the basket into the air fryer. Cook at the corresponding preset mode or Air Fry at 325F (163C) for 6 minutes.

4. After 5 minutes, detach from the air fryer. Set the cheese and diced ham on top and continue cooking for an additional 1 minute.

5. When cooking is processed, the egg should be set and the cheese should be melted. Remove the toast from the air fryer to a plate and let cool for 5 minutes

Nutrition: Calories 184 Fat 11 g Carbohydrates 5 g Sugar 1 g Protein 12 g Cholesterol 0 mg

French toast Casserole

Preparation time: 5 minutes

Cooking time: 12 minutes

Servings 6

Ingredients:

- 3 large eggs, beaten
- 1 cup whole milk
- 1 tablespoon pure maple syrup
- 1 teaspoon vanilla extract
- 1/4 teaspoon cinnamon
- 1/4 teaspoon kosher salt
- 3 cups stale bread cubes
- 1 tablespoon unsalted butter, at room temperature

Directions:

1. In a medium bowl, merge together the eggs, milk, maple syrup, vanilla extract, cinnamon and salt. Stir in the bread cubes to coat well.

2. Grease the bottom of a sheet pan with the butter. Spread the bread mixture into the pan in an even layer.

3. Slide the pan into the air fryer. Cook at the corresponding preset mode or Air Fry at 350F (180C) for 12 minutes.

4. After about 10 minutes, remove the pan and check the casserole. The top should be browned and the middle of the casserole just set. If more time is needed, return the pan to the air fryer and continue cooking.

5. When cooking is complete, serve warm.

Nutrition: Calories 184 Fat 11 g Carbohydrates 5 g Sugar 1 g Protein 12 g Cholesterol 0 mg

French toast Sticks with Strawberry Sauce

Preparation time: 5 minutes

Cooking time: 12 minutes

Servings 4

Ingredients:

1. 3 slices low-sodium whole-wheat bread, each cut into 4 strips
2. 1 tablespoon unsalted butter, melted
3. 1 tablespoon 2 percent milk
4. 1 tablespoon sugar
5. 1 egg, beaten
6. 1 egg white
7. 1 cup sliced fresh strawberries

8. 1 tablespoon freshly squeezed lemon juice

Directions:

1. Arrange the bread strips on a plate and drizzle with the melted butter.

2. In a bowl, whisk together the milk, sugar, egg and egg white.

3. Dredge the bread strips into the egg mixture and place on a wire rack to let the batter drip off. Arrange half the coated bread strips on the sheet pan.

4. Slide the pan into the air fryer. Cook at the corresponding preset mode or Air Fry at 380F (193C) for 6 minutes.

5. After 3 minutes, remove from the air fryer. Use a tong to turn the strips over. Rotate the pan and return the pan to the air fryer to continue cooking.

6. When cooking is processed, the strips should be golden brown. Repeat with the remaining strips.

7. In a small bowl, mash the strawberries with a fork and stir in the lemon juice. Serve the French toast sticks with the strawberry sauce.

Nutrition: Calories 159 Total Fat 11.2 g Saturated Fat 2 g Cholesterol 0 mg Sodium 336 mg Total Carbs 12.3 g Fiber 1.9 g Sugar 9.5 g Protein 1.6 g

Strawberry Toast

Preparation time: 5 minutes

Cooking time: 8 minutes

Servings: 4

Ingredients:

- 4 slices bread, 1/2-inch thick
- 1 cup sliced strawberries
- 1 teaspoon sugar
- Cooking spray

Directions:

1. On a clean work surface, lay the bread slices and spritz one side of each slice of bread with cooking spray.
2. Put the bread slices in the air fryer basket, sprayed side down. Top with the strawberries and a sprinkle of sugar.

3. Slide the basket into the air fryer. Cook at the corresponding preset mode or Air Fry at 375F (190C) for 8 minutes.

4. When cooking is complete, the toast should be well browned on each side. Detach from the air fryer to a plate and serve.

Nutrition: Calories 155 Fat 2 g Carbohydrates 6 g Sugar 2 g Protein 25 g Cholesterol 0 mg

Fast and Easy Cinnamon Toast

Preparation time: 5 minutes

Cooking time: 5 minutes

Servings 6

Ingredients:

- 11/2 teaspoons cinnamon
- 11/2 teaspoons vanilla extract
- 1/2 cup sugar
- 2 teaspoons ground black pepper
- 2 tablespoons melted coconut oil
- 12 slices whole wheat bread

Directions:

1. Merge all the ingredients, except for the bread, in a large bowl. Stir to mix well.

2. Dunk the bread in the bowl of mixture gently to coat and infuse well. Shake the excess off. Arrange the bread slices in the air fryer basket.

3. Slide the basket into the air fryer. Cook at the corresponding preset mode or Air Fry at 400F (205C) for 5 minutes.

4. Flip the bread halfway through.

5. When cooking is complete, the bread should be golden brown.

6. Detach the bread slices from the air fryer and slice to serve.

Nutrition: Calories 245 Fat 15 g Carbohydrates 0.1 g Sugar 0 g Protein 24 g Cholesterol 0 mg

Cinnamon Toast with Strawberries

Preparation time: 15 minutes

Cooking time: 10 minutes

Servings 4

Ingredients:

- 1 (15-ounce / 425-g) can full-fat coconut milk, refrigerated overnight
- 1/2 tablespoon powdered sugar
- 11/2 teaspoons vanilla extract, divided
- 1 cup halved strawberries
- 1 tablespoon maple syrup,
- 1 tablespoon brown sugar, divided
- 1/3 cup lite coconut milk
- 2 large eggs
- 1/2 teaspoon ground cinnamon

- 2 tablespoons unsalted butter, at room temperature
- 4 slices challah bread

Directions:

1. Turn the chilled can of full-fat coconut milk upside down (do not shake the can), open the bottom, and pour out the liquid coconut water. Scoop the remaining solid coconut cream into a medium bowl. Using an electric hand mixer, whip the cream for 3 to 5 minutes, until soft peaks form.

2. Add the powdered sugar and 1/2 teaspoon of the vanilla to the coconut cream, and whip it again until creamy. Place the bowl in the refrigerator.

3. Place the grill plate on the grill position. Select Grill, set the temperature to 450°F (232°C), and set the time to 15 minutes.

4. Merge the strawberries with the maple syrup and toss to coat evenly. Sprinkle evenly with 1/2 tablespoon of the brown sugar.

5. In a large shallow bowl, whisk together the lite coconut milk, eggs, the remaining 1 teaspoon of vanilla, and cinnamon.

6. Place the strawberries on the grill plate. Gently press the fruit down to maximize grill marks. Grill for 4 minutes without flipping.

7. Meanwhile, butter each slice of bread on both sides. Place one slice in the egg mixture and let it soak for 1 minute. Flip the slice over and soak it for another minute. Repeat with the remaining bread slices. Sprinkle each side of the toast with the remaining 1/2 tablespoon of brown sugar.

8. After 4 minutes, remove the strawberries from the grill and set aside. Decrease the temperature to 400F (204C). Place the bread on the grill plate; Grill for 4 to 6 minutes until golden and caramelized. Check often to ensure desired doneness.

9. Set the toast on a plate and top with the strawberries and whipped coconut cream. Drizzle with maple syrup, if desired.

Nutrition: Calories 155 Fat 2 g Carbohydrates 6 g Sugar 2 g Protein 25 g Cholesterol 0 mg

Cornflakes Toast Sticks

Preparation time: 10 minutes

Cooking time: 6 minutes

Servings 4

Ingredients:

- 2 eggs
- 1/2 cup milk
- 1/8 teaspoon salt
- 1/2 teaspoon pure vanilla extract
- 1/3 cup crushed cornflakes
- 6 slices sandwich bread, each slice cut into 4 strips
- Maple syrup, for dipping
- Cooking spray

Directions:

1. Place the crisper tray on the air fry position. Select Air Fry, set the temperature to 390F (199C), and set the time to 6 minutes.
2. In a small bowl, set together the eggs, milk, salt, and vanilla.
3. Put crushed cornflakes on a plate or in a shallow dish.
4. Dip bread strips in egg mixture, shake off excess, and roll in cornflake crumbs.
5. Spray both sides of bread strips with oil.
6. Put bread strips in crisper tray in a single layer.
7. Air fry for 6 minutes or until golden brown.
8. Repeat steps 5 and 6 to air fry remaining French toast sticks.
9. Serve with maple syrup.

Nutrition: Calories 525 Fat 25g Carbs 34g Protein 41g

Mushroom and Squash Toast

Preparation time: 10 minutes

Cooking time: 10 minutes

Servings 4

Ingredients:

- 1 tablespoon olive oil
- 1 red bell pepper, cut into strips
- 2 green onions, sliced
- 1 cup sliced button or cremini mushrooms
- 1 small yellow squash, sliced
- 2 tablespoons softened butter
- 4 slices bread
- 1/2 cup soft goat cheese

Directions:

1. Brush the crisper tray with the olive oil.
2. Place the crisper tray on the air fry position. Select Air Fry, set the temperature to 350F (177C), and set the time to 7 minutes.

3. Put the red pepper, green onions, mushrooms, and squash inside the crisper tray and give them a stir. Air fry for 7 minutes or the vegetables are tender, shaking the crisper tray once throughout the cooking time.

4. Remove the vegetables and set them aside.

5. Spread the butter on the slices of bread and transfer to the crisper tray, butter-side up. Air fry for 3 minutes.

6. Remove the toast from the grill and top with goat cheese and vegetables. Serve warm.

Nutrition: Calories 136 Fat 12.6 g Carbohydrates 4.1 g Sugar 0.5 g Protein 10.3 g Cholesterol 88 mg

Cheesy Crab Toasts

Preparation time: 10 minutes

Cooking time: 5 minutes

Servings 15 to 18

Ingredients:

- 1 (6-ounce / 170-g) can flaked crab meat, well drained
- 3 tablespoons light mayonnaise
- 1/4 cup shredded Parmesan cheese
- 1/4 cup shredded Cheddar cheese
- 1 teaspoon Worcestershire sauce
- 1/2 teaspoon lemon juice
- 1 loaf artisan bread, French bread, or baguette, cut into 3/8inch-thick slices

Directions:

1. Place the crisper tray on the bake position. Select Bake, set the temperature to 360F (182C), and set the time to 5 minutes.

2. In a large bowl, merge together all the ingredients except the bread slices.

3. On a clean work surface, lay the bread slices. Spread 1/2 tablespoon of crab mixture onto each slice of bread.

4. Arrange the bread slices in the crisper tray in a single layer. You'll need to work in batches to avoid overcrowding.

5. Bake for 5 minutes until the tops are lightly browned.

6. Bring to a plate and repeat with the remaining bread slices.

7. Serve warm.

Nutrition: Calories: 374 Total Fat: 16g Saturated Fat: 4g Cholesterol: 62mg Sodium: 254mg Carbohydrates: 38g

Cheesy Chile Toast

Preparation time: 5 minutes

Cooking time: 5 minutes

Servings 1

Ingredients:

- 2 tablespoons grated Parmesan cheese
- 2 tablespoons grated Mozzarella cheese
- 2 teaspoons salted butter,
- 10 to 15 thin slices Serrano chili or jalapeño
- 2 slices sourdough bread
- 1/2 teaspoon black pepper

Directions:

1. Place the crisper tray on the bake position. Select Bake, set the temperature to 325F (163C), and set the time to 5 minutes.

2. In a small bowl, merge together the Parmesan, Mozzarella, butter, and chilies.

3. Scatter half the mixture onto one side of each slice of bread. Sprinkle with the pepper. Place the slices, cheese-side up, in the crisper tray.

4. Bake for 5 minutes, or until the cheese has melted and started to brown slightly.

5. Serve immediately.

Nutrition: Calories: 147 Total Fat: 5g Saturated Fat: 1g Cholesterol: 71mg Sodium: 244mg Carbohydrates: 10g Fiber: 4g Protein: 16g

French toast Sticks

Preparation time: 5 minutes

Cooking time: 12 minutes

Servings: 2 to 4

Ingredients:

- 4 pieces of bread
- 2 tablespoons of butter
- 2 eggs
- 1 pinch of salt
- 1 pinch of cinnamon
- 1 pinch of nutmeg
- 1 pinch of ground cloves
- 1 teaspoon of icing sugar

Directions:

1. Preheat Air-fryer at 180C.Then gently beat together two eggs in a bowl, sprinkle salt, a few heavy shakes of cinnamon, small pinches of both nutmeg and ground cloves.
2. Set both sides of bread slices and cut into strips. Set each strip in the egg mixture and arrange in Air-fryer (cook in two batches).
3. After a period of 2 minutes cooking, pause the Air-fryer to take out the pan, making sure you place the pan on a heat safe surface, spraying the bread with cooking spray.
4. Bring pan to fryer and heat for4 minutes
5. When egg is cooked and bread is golden brown, detach from Air-fryer.
6. Serve immediately and enjoy!

Nutrition: Calories: 244 Fat: 12g Protein: 12g Fiber: 2.4g Carbs: 4.1 g

Mini Pizza

Preparation time: 10 minutes

Cooking time: 29 minutes

Servings 4

Ingredients:

- 1 tsp. of Italian herb seasoning
- 1/4 cup of minced onion
- 6 toasted and split muffins
- 3 tbsp. of steak sauce
- 2 cups of mozzarella cheese
- 1/4 cup of sliced green onion
- 1 can of tomato paste
- 3/4 pound of ground beef
- 2 cups of parmesan cheese

Directions:

1. Crumble meat in a bowl; add onion, tomato paste, Italian herb, and steak sauce.
2. Stir well.
3. Spread the mixture on muffins and transfer to the Air Fryer Grill pan.
4. Set the Air Fryer Grill to pizza function.
5. Cook for about 20 minutes on both sides at 350F.
6. Serve immediately with green onions and cheese.

Nutrition: Calories: 273kcal Fat: 27g Carb: 23g Proteins: 21g

Artichoke with Red Pepper Pizza

Preparation time: 10 minutes

Cooking time: 20 minutes

Servings 1

Ingredients:

- 1 tsp. of dried basil
- 1 can of artichoke hearts
- 1-1/2 cup of mozzarella cheese
- 1 cup of red bell pepper
- 5 cloves of garlic
- Cracked pepper
- 1 tbsp. of olive oil
- 1 pizza shell
- 1 tsp. of oregano
- 1 jar of sliced mushroom

Directions:

1. Mix artichoke hearts, basil, bell pepper, garlic, and cracked pepper in a bowl.
2. Add oregano, mushroom, and olive oil.
3. Place the mixture on the pizza shell
4. Transfer the pizza shell to Air Fryer Grill pan.
5. Set the Air Fryer Grill to pizza function.
6. Cook for about 20 minutes at 350F.
7. Serve immediately

Nutrition: Calories: 359kcal Fat: 18g Carb: 43g Proteins: 12g

Artichoke Turkey Pizza

Preparation time: 10 minutes

Cooking time: 20 minutes

Servings 2

Ingredients:

- 2 cups of chopped cooked turkey
- 1-1/2 cup of mozzarella cheese
- 2 baked pizza crust
- 1 can of black olives
- 1 can of diced tomatoes with garlic, oregano, and basil
- 1/2 cup of shredded parmesan cheese
- 1 can of artichoke hearts

Directions:

1. Place the pizza crusts on a working surface.
2. Place turkey, olive, tomatoes mix, parmesan cheese, olives, and artichokes on them.
3. Transfer the pizza crusts to the Air Fryer Grill pan.
4. Set the Air Fryer Grill to pizza function.
5. Cook for 10 minutes at 450F
6. Serve immediately.

Nutrition: Calories: 196kcal Fat: 7g Carb: 28g Proteins: 8g

Bacon Cheeseburger Pizza

Preparation time: 10 minutes

Cooking time: 20 minutes

Servings 2

Ingredients:

- 6 bacon strips
- 1/2 pound of ground beef
- 1 tsp. of pizza seasoning
- 2 cups of mozzarella cheese
- 2 baked-bread crush
- 20 slices of dill pickles
- 1 chopped small onion
- 2 cups of shredded cheddar cheese
- 8 ounces of pizza sauce

Directions:

1. Set onion and beef over medium heat for about 5 minutes.
2. Drain the meat.
3. Add bacon, seasonings, sauce, cheeses, and pickles.
4. Place the bread crusts on a working surface.
5. Place the ingredients on them.
6. Transfer it to the Air Fryer Grill pan
7. Set the Air Fryer Grill to pizza function.
8. Cook for 10 minutes at 450F

Nutrition: Calories: 322kcal Fat: 12g Carb: 42g Proteins: 17g

Bacon Lettuce Tomato Pizza

Preparation time: 10 minutes

Cooking time: 20 minutes

Servings 2

Ingredients:

- 6 slices of plum tomatoes
- 1 cup of torn romaine lettuce
- 1/3 cup of mayonnaise
- 8 sliced of bacon
- 2 bread shell
- 1 cup of mozzarella cheese

Directions:

1. Spread the bread shell on a working surface.
2. Put mayonnaise, cheese, bacon, and tomatoes on the bread shells.
3. Transfer to the Air Fryer Grill pan.
4. Set the Air Fryer Grill to pizza function.

5. Cook for 17 minutes at 450F.

6. Serve immediately

Nutrition: Calories: 132kcal Fat: 8g Carb: 9g Proteins: 8g

Bread Pudding

Preparation time: 10 minutes

Cooking time: 1 hour 20 minutes

Servings 8

Ingredients:

- 3 eggs
- 2 tbsp. of vanilla
- 3 cups of whole milk
- 3 egg yolks
- 2 tsp. of cinnamon
- 8 tbsp. of butter
- 1 cups of cubed French bread
- 2 cups of granulated sugar
- 1/4 Pyrex bowl

Directions:

1. Mix milk and butter in a bowl and heat in the microwave.
2. Break the egg in another bowl and whisk.

3. Add cinnamon, sugar, eggs, and vanilla.

4. Add the milk mix.

5. Add dried bread; mix until the bread is soaked.

6. Put the mixture in a Pyrex bowl

7. Place the Pyrex bowl on the Air Fryer Grill pan.

8. Set the Air Fryer Grill to bagel/toast.

9. Cook 60 minutes at 270F.

10. Allow cooling before serving

Nutrition: Calories: 379kcal Fat: 8g Carb: 70g Proteins: 9g

Cheesy Bread

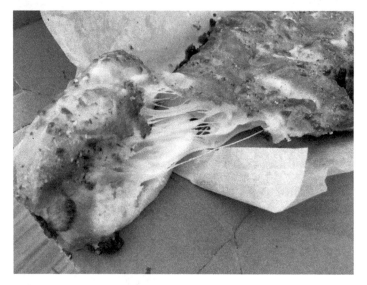

Preparation time: 10 minutes

Cooking time: 20 minutes

Servings 4

Ingredients:

- 4 cloves of garlic
- 1 cup of mozzarella cheese
- 8 slices of bread
- 6 tsp. of sun-dried tomatoes
- 5 tbsp. of melted butter

Directions:

1. Set the bread slices on a flat surface.
2. Put butter on it, garlic, and tomato paste.
3. Add cheese
4. Place the bread on the Air Fryer Grill pan.

5. Set the Air Fryer Grill to toast/bagel function.

6. Cook for 8 minutes a 350F.

Nutrition: Calories: 226kcal Fat: 8g Carb: 32g Proteins: 8g

Breakfast Pizza

Prep and Cooking Time: 10 minutes

Cooking time: 15 minutes

Servings: 5

Ingredients:

- 1 pound of bacon
- 8 ounces of crescent dinner rolls
- 1 cup of cheddar cheese
- 6 eggs

Directions:

1. Place the rolls on the pizza pan.
2. Mix cheese, eggs, and bacon in a bowl.
3. Pour the mixture over the crust.
4. Place the pan in the Air Fryer Grill.
5. Set the Air Fryer Grill to pizza function.

6. Cook for 15 minutes at 370F.

7. Serve immediately

Nutrition: Calories: 311kcal Fat: 11g Carb: 43g Proteins: 15g

French Bread Pizza

Preparation time: 10 minutes

Cooking time: 20 minutes

Servings 2

Ingredients:

- 1 tsp. of dried oregano
- 1/2 cup of fresh mushrooms
- 1 loaf of French bread
- 1/4 cup of parmesan cheese
- 1 cup of mozzarella cheese
- 1/2 green pepper
- 3/4 cup of spaghetti sauce

Directions:

1. Put the spaghetti sauce on the French bread.
2. Add green pepper, cheeses, mushroom, and oregano.
3. Place it on the Air Fryer Grill pan.
4. Set the Air Fryer Grill to pizza function.
5. Cook for 15 minutes at 370F.

Nutrition: Calories: 303kcal Fat: 7g Carb: 51g Proteins: 13g

Vegetable Supreme Pan Pizza

Preparation time: 10 minutes

Cooking time: 30 minutes

Servings 2

Ingredients:

- 8 slice White Onion
- 12 slice Tomato
- 2 tablespoon olive oil
- 3/2 cup shredded mozzarella
- 8 cremini mushrooms
- 1/2 green pepper
- 4 tablespoon Pesto
- 1 Pizza Dough
- 1 cup spinach

Directions:

1. Roll the pizza dough halves until each one reaches the size of the Air Flow racks.
2. Lightly grease both sides of each dough with olive oil.
3. Place each pizza on a rack. Place the racks on the upper and lower shelves of the electric fryer.
4. Press the power button then the French fries button (400 F) and decrease the cooking time to 13 minutes.
5. After 5 minutes, flip the dough onto the top shelf and turn the racks.
6. After 4 minutes, turn the dough onto the top shelf.
7. Take out both racks and drizzle the pizzas with the toppings.
8. Place the racks on the upper and lower shelves of the electric fryer.
9. Press the power button then the French fries button (400 F) and decrease the cooking time to 7 minutes.
10. After 4 minutes, rotate the pizzas.
11. Once the pizzas are done, let them rest for 4 minutes before cutting.

Nutrition: Calories 245 Fat 15 g Carbohydrates 0.1 g Sugar 0 g Protein 24 g Cholesterol 0 mg

Conversion Tables

The unit of measure conversion table is essential in the kitchen when you want to prepare a recipe measured according to a standard different from what you are used to

The recipes are all expressed according to the decimal metric system, but some readers may need to transform them into local measurement systems.

Indeed, some mathematics may be needed initially, but even more, a little logic is necessary because a cup of liquids will weigh differently from a cup of solids, and the same happens with ounces that can measure solid and liquid ingredients.

COOKING CONVERSION CHART

Measurement

CUP	OUNCES	MILLILITERS	TABLESPOONS
8 cup	64 oz	1895 ml	128
6 cup	48 oz	1420 ml	96
5 cup	40 oz	1180 ml	80
4 cup	32 oz	960 ml	64
2 cup	16 oz	480 ml	32
1 cup	8 oz	240 ml	16
3/4 cup	6 oz	177 ml	12
2/3 cup	5 oz	158 ml	11
1/2 cup	4 oz	118 ml	8
3/8 cup	3 oz	90 ml	6
1/3 cup	2.5 oz	79 ml	5.5
1/4 cup	2 oz	59 ml	4
1/8 cup	1 oz	30 ml	3
1/16 cup	1/2 oz	15 ml	1

Temperature

FAHRENHEIT	CELSIUS
100 °F	37 °C
150 °F	65 °C
200 °F	93 °C
250 °F	121 °C
300 °F	150 °C
325 °F	160 °C
350 °F	180 °C
375 °F	190 °C
400 °F	200 °C
425 °F	220 °C
450 °F	230 °C
500 °F	260 °C
525 °F	274 °C
550 °F	288 °C

Weight

IMPERIAL	METRIC
1/2 oz	15 g
1 oz	29 g
2 oz	57 g
3 oz	85 g
4 oz	113 g
5 oz	141 g
6 oz	170 g
8 oz	227 g
10 oz	283 g
12 oz	340 g
13 oz	369 g
14 oz	397 g
15 oz	425 g
1 lb	453 g

CPSIA information can be obtained
at www.ICGtesting.com
Printed in the USA
LVHW012333010821
694126LV00012B/981